SELF ES

GW01453038

A PRACTICAL GUIDE TO UNCONDITIONAL LOVE

JUSTIN ALBERT

WHY YOU SHOULD READ THIS BOOK

This book will help you identify your self esteem and self love levels and boost them to their maximum level. Do you find yourself feeling a lack of confidence in the work place? Do you feel a lack of joy in your personal relationships? Are you unable to like yourself, and do you find yourself consistently stressed and unable to perform well? Your self esteem and self love needs a personalized touch. You must hone your self esteem utilizing the techniques outlined in this book. You must understand that you are simply a person, with very personalized talents and flaws. You must begin to accept yourself for who you are. Only then can you begin to find a better, happier future for yourself.

This book includes an intensive quiz that allows you to diagnose your level of self love and self esteem. It helps you acknowledge where you see yourself in the world. With your score in hand, you can begin applying the book's self esteem techniques. Furthermore, you can study scientific, psychologically-tested research about humans from all over the world. Via this research, you will understand that self esteem is tested in a number of ways. When you understand your stressors, you can begin to hone your self esteem. You can orchestrate your interior mind to become stronger and more successful. You can become the very best version of yourself.

TABLE OF CONTENTS

.

CHAPTER 1. SELF ESTEEM AND SELF LOVE: A CLOSER LOOK AT YOUR LIFE

SELF ESTEEM AND YOUR INTERNAL DIALOGUE

Self esteem is your appraisal of your self worth. It is, essentially, how you think you compare to the rest of the world. This appraisal relates to how well you perform at work, at school, in sports, and in relationships. And, for so many people, this outlook is incredibly dreary and inhibiting.

The thoughts you have about yourself, your inner-dialogue you experience every day, tend to fluctuate. This is natural. After you do well on a test, for example, you tend to think about how smart you are. You feel like you're on top of the world. You stride through your day unencumbered. And you've earned this feeling: you've worked hard to rise to the top. In the hours after a break up, however, you might feel at the very bottom of a well. You might feel like there's no reason to move forward in your life without the strength of a companion. In this instance, you might say that you have very low self esteem, while after a complete accomplishment, you might say you have very high self esteem. It's true that all of these world events can alter the way you feel about yourself. However, it's not necessarily true that these outside effects alter your interior self esteem and self love. The truth is, your self esteem comes from within you. You have complete and utter control.

1

People with good self esteem and people with poor self esteem experience this normal up and down of their interior dialogue, the voice authorizing them different opinions about themselves, quite differently. For example, if a person has good self esteem, these normal ups and downs don't really affect him. He has a temporary fluctuation; maybe this translates to telling himself he's simply having a bad day. However, he doesn't relate this "bad" day to any other days. He simply rides the "down" day till its completion and waits for an opportunity to live differently. However, a person with ready low self esteem allows these exterior events to affect his interior self esteem and feelings quite rapidly and aggressively. On a day when things don't go quite so well, he feels immediately terrible about himself. And he has to ride out this storm for several days until something good happens and he can allow his interior dialogue to ramp up a little bit, restoring him.

Maintaining healthy self esteem allows you to see yourself completely as you are and accept yourself as that person. It allows you to understand your strengths and your weaknesses while still maintaining your feelings of being worthwhile. Holding poor self esteem forces you into the depths of feeling; it forces you to rely on compliments from friends, from day-to-day accomplishments. And these feelings don't last long enough for you to live off of them forever. You must hone your self esteem and become happier with who you are as a complete person. You must build yourself from the inside before you can take on the greater exterior world.

THE DIFFERENCE BETWEEN SELF ESTEEM AND SELF LOVE

Good self esteem allows you to see your abilities and accomplishments as worthwhile aspects of yourself. You are proud of yourself, and you accept yourself for who you are. However, good self esteem may exist in only one area of your life. For example, you may have really good self esteem at work. You know you're the best at a particular element of your job and that you bring your best to work every single day. You know that people notice. And: you also accept, in this work environment, that you could never do what the person across the hall does. You have your unique abilities at work, and that person has his.

For some reason, however, self esteem doesn't always translate across all areas of your life. If you have good self esteem at work, you might still have poor self esteem about what you look like, for example. Perhaps you've never regarded yourself as a particularly attractive individual. And because of this, you don't always treat yourself well. You don't eat well; you don't exercise. And you're spiraling your body down into poor health. You don't have the self esteem to treat yourself properly.

Quit neglecting yourself in those areas of your life in which you don't hold high self esteem. Accept yourself for who you are in every single element of your life, and allow yourself to grow. You must make a commitment, beyond the realms of work, school, relationships, and life endeavors, to love yourself. Breathe love to yourself even in the moments before you get out of bed in the morning. Meditate about yourself, about the ways in which you can

3

accept yourself. Affirm yourself with happy feelings, and look to all the beautiful things in your world: things that you get to appreciate every single day. Only if you work through the very specific elements included later in this book, can you achieve this self love.

And self love builds itself through every area of your life. You'll become an even better, more confident person at work—yes, the place you already feel quite at home in. And you'll begin to treat your body better, eat healthier. You'll feel yourself making a commitment to yourself in so many different elements of your life: because you have given yourself the ability to try.

REASONS FOR A LACK OF SELF LOVE

Your low self esteem and self love has multiple sources. But the truth seems undeniable for everyone. You walk into your adult life with a pre-ordained view of your self worth. Events in your childhood instilled this in you, and you must work to refute your negative feelings. Only then can you assign yourself a better, stronger self worth. Only then can you survive in the rollicking adult world.

1. YOUR AUTHORITY FIGURES OR PARENTS.

It's easy to blame your parents for everything. But it's true that your authority figures growing up had a real hand in creating your view of your self worth.

A. Your parent could have told you, over and over again, that what you did was never good enough. This excessive criticism has made you believe that nothing in your adult life is good enough either. You are never confident in your body and seem to expect failure around every corner. This failure, however, is always crippling no matter how many times you've failed before. You don't exactly get used to it.

B. Alternately, your parents could have been uninvolved or somehow out of the picture. If you didn't have someone there charging your forward and cheering you on, it was difficult for you to learn how to push yourself. Your achievements went unnoticed, and you therefore stopped looking to achieve them. You felt unrecognized, and in your adult life, you feel like you must continually apologize for the fact that you exist.

C. Alternately, your parents could have fought often. When your parents demonstrated their negative feelings toward each other, you probably picked some of those emotions up. As a child, you felt like you contributed to the fighting in one way or another. You felt involved, tainted. And you carried these feelings into adulthood.

2. BULLYING.

Outside of your home environment as a child, you were faced with an entire world of people. And when these people began to demonstrate the inherent cruelty of the world, your self esteem began to take form. If your parents were over-supportive in the face of your external world's bullying, you were unable to develop a layer of protection. Eventually, you began to hide from the world. You saw that your parent's positive thoughts about you were in stunning contrast to what you thought the rest of the world thought about you. You brought these feelings into your adulthood, and you default to a negative idea of yourself.

Alternately, if you were bullied and you had uninvolved parents, you probably felt undeserving of any sort of notice. You felt the lack of safety of the world, and you felt like there was nowhere to turn.

3. INTENSE CHILDHOOD TRAUMA.

Emotional, sexual, or physical abuse can affect children in a variety of ways; most notably, these events can spark incredibly low self esteem. If this happened to you, you probably have a lack of trust for the world. You blamed yourself for the past assaults even though they were not your fault, and today you are unable to feel in control of your surroundings. You view yourself as a shameful entity for having such a past. You do not find yourself worthy of a better future.

4. MEDIA AND SOCIETY.

The world of airbrush in the media is a dark place indeed. It's building a world of false ideas about beauty. You begin to feel like you can't measure up to society's level of beauty. If your original ideas of your self esteem stem from a different place, like a poor childhood, these ideas can manifest themselves in images of media and society.

The causes of low self esteem bind to you as an adult and tend to bring you down and alter your perception of yourself. Try to wield these thoughts away from you. Try

Self Esteem and Self Love

to recognize yourself as a worthwhile human being, and remember that everyone has negative pasts. The more you understand the feelings you have about your past, the better you can refute them and move on to a better future.

CHAPTER 2. IDENTIFY YOUR LOW SELF ESTEEM: TAKE THE QUIZ

Take the first steps toward a better future and understand if you have low self esteem through the following quiz. Reflect on your daily life, and answer the following questions as honestly as possible.

QUESTION 1: ARE YOU A SHY PERSON? DO YOU TEND TO APPROACH PEOPLE FIRST, OR IS IT GENERALLY THE OTHER WAY AROUND?

A) I tend to hang back in a conversation and allow the other person to make the first move. I don't actively give out information about myself. In essence, I am incredibly shy.

B) My shyness depends on my mood—and my alcohol intake.

C) I can be shy around groups of people I don't know; however, once I am comfortable around people, I can't shut up.

D) I almost always strike up a conversation with groups of people I don't know, and I'm always blabbering away about my personal life. Of course, that doesn't mean I'm annoying or anything. I'm simply very easy to talk to, and I like to speak with people of all kinds.

QUESTION 2: DO YOU FEEL THAT, GENERALLY, YOU DISLIKE YOURSELF?

A) I don't like anything about myself, really.

B) I really dislike myself most days. However, I have days when I'm with certain people or achieve certain things. On these days, I allow myself to feel a little bit better about myself.

C) I feel all right about myself. I know I struggle in some areas; for example, I don't really like the way I look in my old high school skirt right now. But over all, I like what I'm doing in my life.

D) I like myself. I'm good at most everything I try; and if I'm not, I know how to work hard to achieve my goals.

QUESTION 3: DO YOU FIND YOURSELF A CONFIDENT INDIVIDUAL?

A) I don't tend to try new things; I don't approach new people or situations. I try to stay at home as often as I can. I lack confidence to move forward in my life.

B) I feel confident in one or two areas of my life. For example, I really like one aspect of my appearance, like my hair, and do a lot to take care of it. However, I don't feel confident at work and often make mistakes because of nerves.

C) I have felt confident in the past; however, an unfortunate recent event, like losing my job, has forced me to reduce my confidence level and feel sort of afraid about moving forward.

D) I don't allow fear to affect my daily life. I am confident and ready for new experiences at all times.

QUESTION 4: DO YOU FEEL LIKE OTHER PEOPLE LIKE YOU?

A) I generally feel like I make a bad first impression and that other people don't want to continue speaking with me after our first encounter. I don't think people like me very much. It could be for any reason.

B) I have a few very close friends that I've had for a long time. I know they like me, although I'm not sure why. As far as everyone else: I don't tend to talk to many new people. I feel like I get strange looks often.

C) I know that I am likable and lovable; however, I do make an ass of myself sometimes. This probably makes a few people not like me as much as I'd like.

D) I am likable. People tend to like me when they first meet me, and I never lose friends.

QUESTION 5: WHEN BAD THINGS HAPPEN TO YOU, DO YOU TEND TO BELIEVE IT'S YOUR FAULT?

A) When bad things happen in my life, I know they reflect exactly how I handled the situation. I messed something up; I failed. If someone else had been handling it, nothing would have gone wrong.

B) I tend to blame myself when bad things happen; I also tend to blame other people. I know that people make mistakes all the time. However, I am able to learn a little bit from my mistakes to better the future.

C) I know that when I fail, I somehow contributed to that failure. However, I know I can find a way to make tomorrow a little bit better by working toward a better future with the knowledge I gained.

D) Other factors obviously went into my bad performance. I practiced the best I could. And it didn't work out. I'll do differently next time. Plus: everyone makes mistakes.

QUESTION 6: DO YOU SEE YOURSELF MORE AS A LEADER, OR MORE AS A FOLLOWER?

A) I have never been a leader. I simply trust other people's opinions more, and I like to follow. It's nice not having everyone rely on me.

B) I've led before, but it was hectic and hard. I definitely failed. It's better for me, these days, to take the sidelines and let other people fail for me.

C) I'm both a leader and a follower. I don't mind when other people are leading, and I take to their opinions well. Also, I like leading. I have good, strong opinions and ideas, and I think people appreciate them.

D) I'm quite often a leader. I have good ideas, and other

people tend to listen to me. I don't take well to following as I feel that it diminishes me as a person.

QUESTION 7: DO YOU FIND YOURSELF STRUGGLING WITH SAYING THE WORD "NO" OFTEN?

A) I almost never say "No," even if I don't want to do something. I want to be everything for everyone at all times.

B) I say "No" only if I know that person I'm refusing will love me or appreciate me anyway. If they're going to lose their respect for me, then I have to say: "Yes."

C) I alternate between "Yes" and "No," of course. It's freeing saying the word "No," but I still find myself agreeing to things out of a sort of guilt.

D) I find myself saying "Yes" less and less. If I don't want to do something or if it isn't my idea, I don't see any reason to do it. I understand that even if I can't do something, I'm not a bad person or anything. I simply don't have the time, or it's not my prerogative.

QUESTION 8: DO YOU FIND YOURSELF LINGERING ON IN BAD RELATIONSHIPS FOR FAR TOO LONG?

A) I never get out of bad relationships until the other person does the "dumping."

B) I have a really great feeling of indifference when it comes to my bad relationship, so much so that I'll just wait until the other person dumps me. It'll happen eventually, but I'd rather not perpetuate the problems.

C) I do tend to linger in relationships a bit too long, but who doesn't? Usually, the right path is decided. And I do the initiating if I have to.

D) Once I figure out the relationship is over, I get out of there. There's no use hanging around and ruining each other's lives with cruel comments and the like. We were meant for better things.

QUESTION 9: DO YOU SUPPRESS YOUR ANGER ONLY TO ERUPT AFTER A WHILE WITH A SORT OF TANTRUM?

A) I find myself keeping my anger inside for a long period of time. Suddenly, when I reach the tipping point, I feel like I go crazy. I lash out at the person who caused my anger.

B) I often work through my anger by writing in a diary or talking to a side friend. However, if I feel that I need to give a person a sort of retribution, the anger suddenly bursts from me a few weeks later. I let things build.

C) I occasionally find myself bottling my anger, but I try to talk my anger or unrest out with the person its involved with. I find that I am able to digest the situation better. Plus, I've seen what happens when I blow up after bottling my anger, and it's not pretty.

D) I am always very open about my emotions. I deal with them objectively, and pass through them. I do not allow my anger to affect my future relationships.

QUESTION 10: DO YOU FIND IT DIFFICULT TO GIVE CRITICISM TO SOMEONE IN PERSON?

A) I never criticize anyone because I feel like they will turn their criticisms back at me. What a scary thought.

B) If my work or friend role requires me to criticize, I do so via email or text message. I avoid face-to-face criticism.

C) I'll give a criticism to someone if I'm absolutely required, face-to-face. For example, if I must at my job, I will. But I won't do it in my personal life as much unless I feel entirely sure of myself in the relationship.

D) I am open and honest in my criticisms. I am, of course, open and honest with my positive points on that person as well. I think it's best to keep everything balanced and to allow other people to understand your stance on things.

ANALYZING YOUR TEST RESULTS

If you answered mostly A's and B's, you have pretty low general self esteem. You are unable to keep your spirit light in situations, and you cannot understand yourself as a human among other fallible humans. Because of this, you are unable to forgive yourself of past mistakes.

Furthermore, you are incredibly shy and are unable to make good friends and push yourself to formulate strong romantic relationships. You lack the confidence to move forward at your work position. Generally, you waste a lot of time worrying if what you've done was correct or right; you spend a lot of time wondering if other people think you're "all right." Your work life and relationship life are suffering due to your bouts of low self esteem.

If you answered mostly C's and D's, on the other hand, you have pretty strong self esteem. You are able to acknowledge that your mistakes are unrelated, that you are just a human with the very real affinity to fail. You aren't very shy, and find yourself worthy of human relationships. You are fruitful in those relationships because you do not bottle up your anger and you are open and honest about your needs. You will go far in your work life, as well, because you have the confidence to succeed. You respect yourself and make good choices for your body. It's important to note that your self esteem is not too high; you know you make mistakes, and you work hard to do better in the future. You acknowledge yourself as a whole person, toned with both strengths and weaknesses. Just like everyone else.

If you fell on the low side of things or slightly in the middle, don't worry. Self esteem can be built utilizing several of the techniques outlined in this book. You can build self esteem just as you would a muscle. But you must exercise it. You must tone it. Pretty soon, other people will recognize your "muscle" of self esteem as well. You'll look strong and confident; you'll be on the road to recovery. Don't ever forget this moment: the moment you decide to push past your low self esteem

15

and build yourself a better life. Rejuvenation and better life construction exists in your future. Go grab it.

TYPICAL AILMENTS OF THE LOW SELF ESTEEM PERSON

Low self esteem affects millions of people in numerous different ways. Uncertainty about how you fit into your surroundings, into your relationships, and in your work life is not the tipping point.

People suffering from low self esteem can experience:

1. Depression.
2. Eating disorders like Bulimia nervosa or Anorexia nervosa.
3. Social phobia.
4. Drug abuse.
5. Alcohol abuse.
6. Relationship problems; a lack of ability to find happiness with another.
7. Self-hate.
8. Anxiety.

THE THREE REPRESENTATIVES OF LOW SELF ESTEEM

Self esteem is often running rampant through people you interact with every single day. Sometimes, it's hard to remember that these people may be dealing with interior unrest and low self esteem. However, you can look for these three "faces" of poor self esteem represented on the street today.

1. *THE VICTIM.*

   You've probably spoken to a "victim" before. The victim with poor self esteem acts utterly helpless in every situation. He or she is waiting for someone else to come and change his life. He's not making changes in his life to better himself, and he's utilizing self-pity or a sort of indifference about his situation in order to cope. He looks to everyone else around him for guidance and for advice. With this repeated search for assistance, he tends to be unassertive, completely reliant, and revel in underachievement. His relationships are generally one-sided because he cannot be his full, upright self.

2. *THE REBEL.*

   The rebel with low self esteem works through his feelings with anger. He does not have respect for the good will or the opinions of the people around him, and he lacks the ability to look at the world as a good place. He feels angry about not living up to his potential, but he acts with a feeling of indifference about this. He also must prove that his peers' opinions about him, their criticisms, don't hurt him. By doing this, he tends to break rules or laws, blame others for his problems, and oppose all authority.

3. *THE IMPOSTER.*

   The imposter is the hardest of all low self esteem faces to spot in the crowd. The person with low self esteem, in this case, acts incredibly happy and tends to have many accomplishments. However, he lives with the constant fear of failure. He feels that he might be found out to be a failure living in a world of success; and therefore, he relies on constant success in order to prove himself. He holds several problems relating to procrastination, perfectionism, burn-out, and severe competition.

Chapter 3. Psychological Self Esteem and Self Love Research

Several studies about self esteem have been conducted throughout the years, yielding incredible understanding about the human environment and human needs. It's important to study what has been learned so that you can conduct yourself differently than the "norm," if possible, and also acknowledge that your weaknesses in your self esteem are found in everyone else. This way, you don't have to spiral out of control.

Professional Competition and Male and Female Romantic Relationships

Recent research made an incredible discovery. According to a study conducted by American Psychological Association, men with successful wives or girlfriends often do not relate to the joy felt by their partner. Instead, their self esteem drops dramatically. According to the study, it didn't matter what the wife or girlfriend was good at. She could be good at academia; she could be a wonderful hostess. Regardless, men had higher self esteem when their female partner failed rather than when she succeeded. Women, on the other hand, were not affected by their male partner's successes or failures. It seems unique to men. The research shows that men find women's success as automatic competition to their own success.

The American Psychological Association studied 896 people over the course of five experiments to bring their results.

One of the experiments brought together thirty-two couples from the University of Virginia. The couples were given a test that was said to be a test about problem solving and general intelligence. After the test, each person "learned" that his or her partner had scored in either the top twelve percent or bottom twelve percent of university students. When asked, face-to-face, what they felt about their partner's success or failure, each person said generally the same things. What they said, vocally, was not affected.

However, the participants were also given a test to peg how each of them felt, on a subconscious level, about his or her partner's success. The test was on the computer, and it tracked word association with self esteem. For example, when someone saw the word "me," he or she could match this with the words "good" or "bad" and all of their associated words.

The results of the test were dramatic. The men who had learned that their woman partner had tested in the top twelve percent of everyone at university scored significantly lower on their self esteem test.

In a different study, women were shown to actually feel better about their relationships with men when their men had succeeded. Men, on the other hand, tended to feel worse about their relationships when their women had succeeded.

WHAT CAN WE LEARN?

From this study, men can learn to be more conscious of their reaction to their female counterpart's success. If you are a man and you find yourself in the realm of a successful woman, try your best to actually feel happy for her success. Understand that she would feel utter joy for you if you were successful. Try to eliminate your feelings of competition and remember that everyone has different skills. Your wife or girlfriend has found hers, and that reflects well on you, as an individual, as well. Not only have you found a remarkable partner; you have also found a remarkable partner who has chosen you for her partner. Someone incredibly successful thinks you're wonderful. And that should be all you need to know.

Self Esteem and External Sources

A study by the American Psychological Association analyzed the relationship between your self esteem and its basis on what other people think about you. They found that basing your self esteem on other people's opinions actually boosted your chance of mental and physical problems. The study found that college students who based their self esteem and self worth on things like their appearance and their popularity reported signs of anger, stress, relationship conflicts, and higher usage of drugs and alcohol. Furthermore, they were at higher risk of eating disorders.

The study surveyed six hundred students. It surveyed the college students three times: once in the summer right before their first year of college, once at the end of their first fall semester, and once at the end of their first spring semester. A great majority of the students, rather surprisingly, had high self esteem. However, the students generally based this self worth on their academic competence, their ability to do better than their peers, their support from their family, and their appearance.

Throughout the year, it was found that the students who based their self esteem and worth on their school performance did not actually receive higher grades than the other students. These students who based their self worth on their academic success reported great strain with professors and dire stress in times of tests.

It was found that students who based their self worth on things that reflected on themselves: these things like academic performance, appearance, etc., had a greater risk of stress and fear of failure. They felt anxious the entire year. On the other hand, the students who based their self worth on things like moral standards or simply being good to others had a lower rate of alcoholism and eating disorders.

The conclusion of the American Psychological Association was that students should make goals regarding things greater than themselves. They should think about what they can create with their abilities rather than how their abilities reflected upon them as individuals.

WHAT CAN WE LEARN?

As you build your self esteem, it's important that you don't build yourself up with external things. Don't build your self worth with how well you did at work that day, for example, or how great your hair looked. These things will only make you feel terrible when your hair doesn't fall exactly right the next day, or your meeting doesn't go as planned in the following week. Instead, match your self worth against interior emotions. Allow yourself to feel that your goals are resoundingly best for society and that you're looking to better something greater than yourself.

CHILD PRAISE AND SELF ESTEEM ISSUES

New research from the American Psychological Association shows that when you praise young children with low self esteem—most notably, when you praise them for their personal qualities rather than their efforts—they are more susceptible to negative feelings and fear of failure. Therefore, when you praise a child for how well he did on his spelling test rather than how hard he worked on his spelling test, you may be annihilating any good you might have done with your praise. Personal praise may backfire.

The experiment brought together 357 Netherland parents from the ages of 29 to 66. They read descriptions of six hypothetical children. Three of these children had high self-esteem. For example, the description said something like: "Margot often liked the person she was." The other three had low self esteem For example, the description said something like: "Lisa didn't really like herself." Afterwards, the parents were meant to write down what sort of praise they would lend the child after he or she completed a specific assignment, like drawing. Through this, the study showed that the parents were far more likely to give personal quality praise to low self esteem children than high self esteem children. They tended to give high self esteem children more effort-based praise. For example, they might say that they "did a good job of singing that song," rather than "your voice is really pretty."

Another experiment illustrated the children's self esteem quite well. Children from the Netherlands between the ages of 8 to 13 were made to take a standardized test that measured their self esteem. Afterwards, they were brought to computer screens to play a computer game. The children were told that they would be playing against children at a different school. This was, of course, not true. The computer actually controlled who won or lost the game. Afterwards, one group of children received the praise: "Wow, you're great!" This was a personal praise. Another group of children received the praise: "Wow, you did good work!" This was praise in relation to the children's efforts. The final group was the control, and they received no praise

Afterwards, the children were told to complete a second round. They were told, at the end, whether or not they won or lost. Then, they took a survey about how they felt. The children who lost the game and ALSO had been praised on their PERSONAL worth experienced the highest level of shame.

WHAT CAN WE LEARN?

Praising someone's self worth can negatively affect his feelings of self esteem and self love. While you might not think there's a big difference between "Wow, you're wonderful!" and "Wow, you did a great job back there!," the differences are powerful. When you relate the person inside to the exterior events, you link their happiness levels with things they cannot control. He can feel shame much more easily, and this can spiral his self esteem and self confidence into the depths.

FACEBOOK AND SELF ESTEEM

Facebook's been around something, and it seems like it's here to stay. Most of you probably spend at least a few minutes on it a day, checking out your friend's status updates and figuring out precisely what you missed last night when you stayed inside to binge-watch Mad Men instead. A recent study conducted at the University of Gothenburg in Sweden has created a link between low self esteem and Facebook, ultimately giving a shove to these "virtual" relationships everyone seems to have.

The university studied 1,011 people with an average of about thirty-two years of age. The study analyzed what users find important with regards to their Facebook utilization. They further analyzed how, exactly, the users portrayed themselves via their status updates. They used this information to yield a link between Facebook and self esteem.

They found, without surprise, that eight-four percent of the people in the study used Facebook every single day. They spent about 75 minutes per day on Facebook, on average.

The results showed that the users who spent the most time of Facebook had the least amount of self esteem.

Generally, women had greater self esteem issues than men with regards to the Facebook research. Men were generally unaffected by Facebook, and their happiness with their lives was not altered by the dreaded news feed.

WHAT CAN WE LEARN?

Get off the social networking sights and see people face-to-face. The study showed that the men tended not to speak about their problems on Facebook, thus allowing them to go into the world and speak through their problems to an actual person. This is much healthier. On the other hand, women were much more likely to talk about their problems on Facebook, thus bringing their problems to their internal mind and compartmentalizing them.

Work through your problems with an actual person. Deal with your feelings in a different manner, and try to limit your Facebook usage. Comparing yourself to other people doesn't do you any good, and their lives are brought to you through a very skewed camera. Remember that.

Chapter 4. Self Love: Loving Yourself Can Revitalize Your Love of Others

Self Love and Self Compassion

Having self love and compassion allows you to bring the same care and attention to yourself that you bring to other people. For some reason, it is far more natural to care for friends and family, to ask after their sickness or break up, to give them a much-needed relief from the tremors of their life, than it is to give yourself a break. You must begin to empathize with your own feelings. Your feelings demonstrate themselves in countless ways and affect your day-to-day life endlessly. If you stop inhibiting your feelings or otherwise putting them down, you may begin to grow beyond the stagnation of your feelings. In other words, when you stop dragging yourself down and telling yourself how much you "can't" do something, you'll finally have the ability and the strength to do it.

As aforementioned, this feeling of self love is overarching. It reaches beyond the realms of each of your areas of self esteem. For example, if you have remarkable self esteem and good feelings about your work life, that doesn't mean you have proper self esteem about your own body. You avoid mirrors, for example, and tell yourself how much you don't deserve something—especially on certain diet plans. However, you must begin to bring this idea of self love into your life so that you can revitalize your self esteem. Your self love will allow you to make good, nourishing choices for your body. You will begin to like your body, and you will want it to do good things for you. Therefore, you administer fruits and vegetables and protein to fuel it. You recognize the relationship between your body and your mind. And your self love demonstrates itself in this nourishing arena.

LOW SELF ESTEEM AND RELATIONSHIPS

It's clear that when people have low self esteem, they attempt to receive affirmation of their good values via their personal relationships. They require the relationship to see themselves as accepted in the greater world. However, this leads to insecurities in the relationship. People with low self love and self esteem who cannot love themselves are unable, therefore, to bring about the same love and esteem in their partner. Low self love can become like a barrier between two people.

Oftentimes, the following barriers get in the way of a relationship wrought with self doubt and insecurities:

1. LOW SELF ESTEEM PERSON ASSUMES THE WORST.

People with low self esteem generally want their partners to see them as better, more intelligent, and more compassionate people than they see themselves. However, in a recent study, it was shown that partners with low self-esteem underestimated the ways in which their partners saw them on an incredible level. On the other hand, people with high self esteem were able to have an accurate reading on how their partners saw them.

2. CONDITIONAL LOVE ASSUMPTION IS FRIGHTENING.

As outlined previously, anything during the low self esteem person's day can trigger a negative reaction. For example, if he loses his job, his self worth for that day is on a negative slide. He takes these exterior events to mean that he, himself, is bad. He reflects bad events on his personality. He requires his partner, of course, to see beyond the rubbish; he requires his partner to understand that he is not a mirror of his failure. He didn't fail because of something inside of himself; he didn't fail because of his worth. However, he fears that when he seeks his partner to assist him with these feelings, his partner will no longer love him the same way.

Usually, when the partner tries to point out that the event was exterior, that he was not to be blamed for the incident, the person with low self esteem simply states that he does not believe his partner. He becomes critical of what his partner is saying about him, and in return his partner becomes withdrawn. Of course, this was what the low self esteem person was fishing for all along. He thought he wouldn't be loved; and now he is feeling unloved.

The positive partner must attempt to always take the high ground in this regard. Always stick with the "I am still in love with you despite this thing that happened to you" approach.

3. CONTAMINATING THE PARTNER'S OPINION.

Oftentimes, people with low self esteem will try to think poorly of their partners because of their partner's high opinion of them. In a way, this is a sort of self protection. The people with low self esteem don't feel themselves worthy of a relationship, and thus they try to refute the relationship with all they can. They question their partner's positivity and try to diminish their partner's need for them. For the partner with high self esteem, this is incredibly insulting. To the partner with low self esteem, this is dangerous. They're attempting to protect themselves from a break up by perhaps making the break up happen early. However, their surge from the relationship will not boost them into any sort of bright reality.

LEARN TO BUILD A BETTER RELATIONSHIP

A recent study found that people with high self esteem did not alter their perceptions and opinions of their partners when they remembered a past transgression enacted by the partners. Instead, they understood that their love for them was compatible with the mistakes that partner had made. They understood that love was imperfect, just like the rest of the world—and just like themselves. Their standards are lower, and thus their quality of life is higher. This is not because they have a worse-off life, of course. Instead, their life is vibrant because they understand that imperfections stand at every corner. They forgive themselves, on an internal level, for their mistakes.

Having a partner either with high self esteem or low self esteem can help you, if you have low self esteem, build a better future for yourself. You walked into your adult like with low self esteem, and this is not altogether your fault. Your childhood, your past was ripe with errors all around, and you did not leave unscathed. However, having a relationship can help you hold a different perspective of yourself.

Each day, list something positive about yourself and something positive about your partner. These positive remarks don't have to be related. Bring a different idea of trust into your relationship by yielding a concrete understanding of it to yourself. Understand that relationships are beautiful when you love yourself because you can fuel more love into your shared situation. And that person, your partner, can give you the much-needed boost you need to fuel you for the other parts of your life.

CHAPTER 5. STEPS TO BETTER LIFE FULFILLMENT AND SELF LOVE

1. ## BEGIN TO ANALYZE YOUR INTERIOR DIALOGUE MUCH MORE HARSHLY AND TAKE STEPS TO CHANGE IT.

Your interior dialogue follows you throughout your life and tends to alter the ways in which you proceed through every event. Therefore, it's best to have a thriving inner voice so that you can approach every situation in a positive manner. With a positive interior dialogue, you can appreciate every moment completely.

Your inner voice may be many things.

A. THE HARSH INNER CRITIC.

Your harsh inner critic steps in after you've completed something. For example, your harsh inner critic says something like this:

"They said I did well up there during my piano recital. However, I made so many little mistakes in that one part. I didn't do as well as I practiced last night. I can't believe all the people in the audience didn't comment on how bad I did during that part. I'm an imposter in the greater world of music."

Instead of thinking about all the tiny mistakes, it's better to acknowledge your strengths Force yourself to think something like this:

"Everyone in the crowd really liked it and cheered so much afterwards! I'm so glad they enjoyed it. It wasn't perfect, of course. But I was pretty nervous up there. I practiced very hard for the concert, and I did as well as I could do. I'm proud of my performance."

You must alter the ways you think about your past performances in your life to allow yourself to build up to a better future.

B. THE UNREALISTIC GENERALIZATION INNER VOICE.

Unrealistic generalizations tend to take over your inner dialogue to bring greater depth of unfortunate feelings to a small scenario. For example, your inner voice might sound something like this:

"I failed the exam. I obviously don't understand a single thing in this college course. I am the biggest idiot ever, and I shouldn't even be in college. I'm not fooling anyone. Everyone can see that I should be somewhere else. I'm not cut out for academics."

Instead of generalizing one bad situation and creating greater brevity, try to think about a bad situation like this in a different sort of way:

"I didn't do so well on this exam. And that sucks. However, I've done all the homework, and I've followed several things during the class. Now that I understand how poorly I did on this first exam, I can alter my study habits a little bit to better my chances the next time around. I've worked myself through other hard classes. It's all about confidence and perseverance!"

Don't allow one failure to push you to the brink of poor feelings. Allow yourself to look at each poor experience with an understanding that you can learn from it.

C. AN ILLOGICALLY LEAPING INNER DIALOGUE.

Sometimes if you have poor self esteem, your inner dialogue can make some irrational jumps. For example, you might think:

"Wow. That guy just frowned at me. He didn't say anything to me as he walked by, but I'm sure he thought I was quite ugly. Ugh."

Just because someone frowns at you in the middle of his day doesn't mean he doesn't like you or thinks anything bad about you! He could be all stressed out about something in his own life; he could have low self esteem as well and think that you didn't like him! Regardless, try to analyze the times you think like this and alter them:

"He's frowning at me. But it is probably not because he doesn't like me. He's probably thinking about something he has to do later. Like the dishes. Or laundry. I probably didn't even come into his mind or alter his opinion at all."

D. THE CATASTROPHIC INNER VOICE.

Sometimes, you can experience something bad and take it far too personally, thus pushing yourself away from trying anything new ever again. You can begin to feel like you aren't good enough for anything new! For example:

"I'm so embarrassed. I asked that guy out to dinner, and he said he couldn't. He obviously doesn't like me. And no one likes me. I am unlikable, and I'll never be in a relationship."

Instead, think about the experience of someone turning you down in a more general, objective way.

"Well, that sucked. He doesn't want to date me. However, I have so many good qualities. Sure, they might not align with his idea of what he wants in a partner. And that's okay. That doesn't mean they won't align well with what someone else wants. I'm confident that I can find someone who will like me for who I am."

2. HONE YOUR SELF COMPASSION AND SELF LOVE.

Self compassion is bringing yourself the same empathic feelings that you show others, and you must begin to practice this with greater demonstration. If you saw, for example, that a friend was going through a hard break up, you wouldn't approach her with all of your problems or put her down or otherwise try to make her feel worse. Instead, you'd be more caring; you'd show her your support. Remind yourself to show yourself the same sort of compassion. If you're having a hard time, acknowledge it. Don't focus on how terrible you're doing on something. Instead, nurture yourself, feed yourself good foods, allow yourself some decent sleep. Treat yourself like a person in need of extra care.

A. ALLOW YOURSELF TO FORGIVE YOURSELF.

When things don't go quite as well as you'd hoped in a certain situation, it's quite easy to blame yourself for everything that went wrong. Instead of being critical of yourself, however, you must be gentle with yourself. Forgive yourself and tell yourself that failure is inevitable; it's a part of life.

B. ALLOW YOURSELF TO RECOGNIZE YOUR UTTER HUMANNESS AND IMPERFECTION.

All humans make mistakes. External factors are always at play, impacting your ability to succeed. For example, you might want to win the mini marathon in your city. You've trained for countless days; and yet, when you get there, you don't win. This might be because the person who did win has a more economical physique than you: that is, he can simply run a lot faster than you due to his genetic make up. This is an external factor that you obviously could not control! You must accept your "humanness." You are given a very unique set of genetics that yield a very specific set of skills. You are connected to the rest of humanity because the rest of humanity is quite "human" and prone to failure, as well. You are never experiencing failure alone. Recognizing this allows you to be far more compassionate with yourself.

C. ALLOW YOURSELF BALANCED EMOTIONS.

When you feel upset or angry, try to "feel" these emotions appropriately. Experience your anger or your sadness in a balanced way. Don't suppress the emotions; however, at the same time, don't get swept up in the emotions either. As you practice this "mindfulness," analyzing your emotions as they come, don't judge your negative emotions or make yourself feel worse for having them. Simply analyze them and allow them to pass. Remember, of course, that these emotions are only temporary. The temporary quality of these feelings allows you not to be overwhelmed. It allows you to move forward in your life.

3. ## LOOK TO THE HELP OF OTHERS TO BOOST YOUR SELF CONFIDENCE AND SELF LOVE.

Oftentimes, looking to the strengths and abilities of people in your life can help you stride forward into a better future, a better environment. However, if you're struggling with self esteem issues right now, you may be one of the people in the world who find it most difficult to ask for assistance. You may feel that you don't deserve this assistance; on the other hand, you might feel like you aren't good enough to succeed. Work through these feelings. When you reach out to other people, they can help you revert the very critical feelings you have about yourself—the feelings that tend to come from your past. Try one of the following maneuvers.

A. SPEAK WITH A THERAPIST OR A COUNSELOR.

If your pain from low self esteem is massive and overtaking your life, you might want to look to the professional sect of speakers. Allowing yourself to speak out your problems with a therapist or a counselor can help you to explore your feelings about yourself. Your counselor or therapist can help you analyze the ways you can improve your future. You can improve your self esteem.

B. LOOK FOR SUPPORT FROM YOUR FRIENDS AND FAMILY.

The next time you speak with a friend or family member, ask them to tell you precisely what they like about you or what they feel you often do well. Ask this person to allow you to talk out your feelings and explore them; ask this person not to give any advice, but to listen to you whole-heartedly. Ask for reminders about how much you are loved. You aren't trying to fish for anything; not really. You already know, deep down, that these people care about you and love you. You are simply asking for reminders. If they know you so well, they probably know you suffer from low self esteem. They'll want to help.

C. LOOK TO TEACHERS AND OTHER ADVISORS.

If you're struggling in your work or school life, it's important to take initiative and ask for help. Go to your professor's office and ask him a specific question; go to a tutor and ask him to walk you through the specific steps you must understand in order to pass the class. Ask your boss what you should do better in order to become a more efficient worker for him. These people should be there to guide you, to help you better yourself. Furthermore, you should reach out and try new things to build your confidence. Try taking a swimming class or learning to ballroom dance. Fueling yourself with more information boosts your self esteem and self confidence in marvelous ways.

4. WORK THROUGH YOUR NEGATIVE BODY IMAGE.

A poor body image is linked to low self esteem in a variety of ways. If you don't believe you're worthy of living a fruitful life, for example, you may begin to eat poorly or quit exercising. On the other hand, if you quit exercising and begin to eat poorly, you may develop a poor body image because you don't like what you see in the mirror. This feeling can translate into a self esteem problem. And as we've learned previously, the different areas of your life and the self esteem you feel in these areas are quite readily linked.

A. STOP COMPARING YOURSELF TO OTHERS.

Remember this: everyone has a different genetic make up. It's like we're all a little messed up out of the factory, if you will. We all have a different "problem" just like the toys that don't make it into the store. And that's good, because these appearance problems make us look a little different than everyone else. If you have a bigger nose or if your hair is frizzy, this allows you to have different attributes than your friend Sally, for example, who has long flowing locks but also an unfortunate uni-brow. Note: it is never good to bring up her uni-brow. She knows about it, just like you know about your nose. Appearance quirks are interesting. But they get you nowhere if you begin to compare your appearance quirks to other people with different kind of quirks. You have your own unique strengths. Think about what other people tell you about yourself all the time: that you have a nice smile or your body looks really great in red.

B. BEGIN TO TAKE CARE OF YOUR HEALTH.

When you take care of yourself through exercise and a good diet, the benefits are explosive. You'll begin to feel physically able to proceed with your life on a new level. You'll have strength you didn't know you could have. Try to eat a variety of fruits, vegetables, and proteins, and try to leave processed carbohydrates out of the mix. Research has shown that carbohydrates pack a real punch in both the weight gain department and the depression department.

Furthermore, if you "get sweaty" about three times a week, your body will begin to release endorphins, or "feel-good" hormones. You'll begin to look at the world a little brighter. Also, you'll feel more confident in your clothes and in your body.

C. TAKE CARE OF YOUR EVERYDAY APPEARANCE.

When you have a poor body image, you tend to stop taking good care of yourself. For example, people with poor thoughts about their weight tend to shower entirely less than people with appropriate thoughts about their weight. Begin to make an effort in your daily beauty and appearance routine and put your best face forward. Do three things a day, at least. For example: do something new with your hair, shave, pluck your eyebrows, or comb your hair into a side-part. Acknowledge yourself as a

person with good appearance intentions;
remember that cleanliness is important when you
meet anyone new.

CHAPTER 6. A LOOK AT YOUR FUTURE LIFE: BETTER SELF ESTEEM AND GREATER SELF LOVE

Work toward a better, more productive future with the removal of your self doubt and your poor self esteem. The reasons for your low self esteem and lack of self love are undeniable, rooted in a past too far away to alter. But you must attempt to forget these past events. They do not define you, and they do not reflect your worth. Begin to appraise yourself in relation to your current strengths. Acknowledge your weaknesses as attributes that make you very, very human—just like everyone else.

With proper self love and self esteem, you can look at the world, at your human relationships, and your work life with a renewed sense of confidence. You will find yourself working toward a promotion and understanding that you deserve it. Feeling like you deserve something actually boosts your chances of receiving it; how can you imagine that anyone is more qualified than you or that anyone wants anything more than you? Don't even think of it. Furthermore, if you receive this new, ranked position, your self esteem will allow you to become a better leader. You'll have empathy for both yourself and for your employees. You'll understand what stressors affect you, and you'll give yourself a break when things don't go as planned. Things never really go as planned, do they? Life is more interesting that way.

Treat yourself well. Love yourself, and live in flourishing

relationships. Work toward promotions, and have a fruitful, successful journey. No one else is going to live this life for you. Quit apologizing for yourself and your existence, and remember your inherent "humanness" is really a beautiful thing.

BENEFITS OF HIGH SELF ESTEEM

With strong self esteem sensibilities, you can finally:

1. Have the confidence to work creatively and outside existing boundaries. Not only can you rejuvenate your work life, you can spin it in a way to reflect your unique talents.

2. Maintain wonderful, nourishing relationships. If you are confident, you will attract other confident people. Together, you will create a world of happiness without anxiety.

3. Have the ability to take risks. When you have better self esteem, you'll take greater risks and therefore receive ultimate success. You will no longer fear the failure associated with risk, and you'll take charge of your life.

4. Spend less time worrying. When you have low self esteem, you are constantly worrying about the different results of certain situations. Without worry on your back, you can utilize your energy for greater, more constructive purposes.

5. Take criticism and learn from it. As mentioned in previous posts, when you have self esteem problems, you are unable to accept criticism. Because you able to see

criticism without emotional effects, you can take criticism and build upon it. You can create yourself into a better person.

ABOUT THE AUTHOR

My mission with this is to be able to help inspire and change the world, one reader at a time.

I want to provide the most amazing life tools that anyone can apply into their lives. It doesn't matter whether you have hit rock bottom in your life or your life is amazing and you want to keep taking it to another level.

If you are like me, then you are probably looking to become the best version of yourself. You are likely not to settle for an okay life. You want to live an extraordinary life. Not only to be filled within but also to contribute to society.

OTHER BOOKS BY JUSTIN ALBERT

Personal Growth for Teens: Discover Yourself and Become Who You Want

Personal Growth and Inspiration: Achieve Greatness in Everything You Do

MOTIVATION: *GETTING MOTIVATED, FEELING MOTIVATED, STAYING MOTIVATED*

Confidence: Build Unbreakable, Unstoppable, Powerful Confidence: Boost Your Confidence: A 21-Day Challenge

Spirituality: A Search for Balance and Enlightenment: Spiritual Health and Wellness

FREE PREVIEW OF

MOTIVATION:

GETTING MOTIVATED, FEELING MOTIVATED, STAYING MOTIVATED

JUSTIN ALBERT

WHY YOU SHOULD READ THIS BOOK

Motivation provides ultimate life fulfillment. It is the driving force behind every profession, every physical action. It fuels the creation of towering skyscrapers, five-star restaurant, and stellar paintings—

And yet: why is motivation so difficult to attain and maintain? Another thing: why is it so difficult to get out of bed? When did life get so out of hand?

This book analyzes these questions on both a scientific and emotional level. It lends the proper tools to build motivation in the wake of utter difficulty.

Motivation is pumping in every blood vessel, through every neuron. Human ancestors struggling to survive in the wild were fueled with this instinct: this motivation to persevere. Present people still pulse with this very intrinsic motivation. However, present-day people— because their needs are generally met, their food is generally supplied—must work for their motivation. They must keep eyes open; they must create their own understanding of their goals. Their goal is no longer: survive. Their goal is to prosper.

Procrastination. Stress. The dog needs walking, the cat needs fed. The work piles up, and motivation for desires and interests is simply out of reach. This Motivation E-book teaches the art of catching desires and interests once again and persevering. It outlines the ways one can work through the blocks in your path and attain that promotion, achieve that great legacy. One must do this:

reach for real, vibrant goals in order to attain real destiny—to know self-actualization. Only with self-actualization can one feel a renewed sense of prosperity, a full sense of self.

CHAPTER 1. MOTIVATION: THE ONLY ROAD TO GREATNESS

Humankind's all-inclusive goal is, effectively, one thing: to survive. The survival concept lurks behind all things in a person's life: behind every kitchen product, behind every home improvement store. And yet, naturally, this survival has changed over the years. It has diminished from something broad, something that must meet required caloric values and required habitat-levels into something much more refined.

What is, then, man's essential, present-day goal? To simply live. And to live well. To live better than man has before. And this goal requires innovation; it requires a push against the limits surrounding each person's life. Without breadth of motivation, people would not leave their beds; they wouldn't work to find a better life. Without motivation, people would have nothing.

Motivation is the call to action. It is the thing that pushes one from one's bed to greet the world and squeeze every ounce of energy from it. It is the thing that forces one to take one's proper stance in the world.

Do you feel, today, that you have the depth of motivation to reach your goals, to push yourself to the top of your career and become a prime person—a person with both physical and mental strength? Do you have the will to survive and the motivation to make the most of that survival?

Understand motivation and the current factors blocking you from your complete embrace of your goals. Understand the ways in which you can become the best version of yourself.

WHAT IS MOTIVATION?

Understanding the precise utilization of motivation is essential in order to prescribe everyday life goals; prescribing life goals via motivation allows for forward-motion.

DEFINITION OF MOTIVATION

Motivation, essentially, is that which initiates and maintains goal-driven mannerisms. It is an unseen force. Biological, cognitive, and social effects alter motivation; these forces mold it, form it into something that either allows growth or stagnation.

Biological effects on motivation involve the various mechanisms required at a very physical level. As aforementioned, one has kitchen appliances that rev and whir in order to maintain a very base biological motive: to boost one's caloric intake for further survival. One reaches for a glass of Coca Cola, essentially, out of motivation to quench one's thirst. These motives are incredibly basic and biological; the animals and plants of the earth have similar biological motivations, as well. A human simply has refined his reach to maintain these motivations.

Cognitive effects on motivation are incredibly complicated. Hormonal imbalances, the things one eats and the things by which one is surrounded can affect the
51

brain, thus altering one's motivational output. Depression, stress, and low self-esteems accumulate at this cognitive level and impair judgment, thus altering continued rev for motivation.

Social effects on motivation generally involve one's environment and cultural influence. What is expected of one in one's culture generally contributes to one's sense of motivation; for example, history finds women generally staying home with children. Their motivation could not grow due to social influences. Furthermore, one's parents and one's friends alter social motivation. If one lives in a stagnant environment—an environment featuring people without conscious effort, without conscious forward-motion, one might simply assimilate into this way of life. However, if one's parents expect certain successes, social motivation might be the factor contributing to one's college graduation, for example.

THREE COMPONENTS OF MOTIVATION

1) Activation
2) Persistence
3) Intensity

Activation is the primary component: the decision to begin. A person must make this conscious decision; it is the root of all motivation. It is the very thing that allows mature motivation to grow. For example, actively enrolling in an exercise class activates the motivation to become healthy and lose weight, thus improving one's life.

Persistence is the continuation of this activation. It involves one's push through obstacles after the initial activation. It involves intense, psychological strength. For example, after one enrolls in the exercise class with the obvious intention of becoming healthy and thin, persistence must step in to truly fuel motivation. After the exercise class begins, one must invest endless hours, limitless concentration, and physicality to the point of exhaustion. It is increasingly difficult to maintain the intensity. However, if one is fueled with the proper motivation, working through the exercise class until completion garners significant strength and benefits.

Finally, intensity measures one's level of vigor after initially activating and persisting. If one persists through the various exercise classes, for example, without a significant level of concentration and exertion, one is not truly motivated. One can persist, certainly. But one will not reach the final goal of true health and strength without full-throttle intensity. Find another example in university-level classes. One can activate one's enrollment; one can attend every class; but if one does not fuel every day with study and push one's self outside of class, one will probably not achieve maximum success.

EXTRINSIC MOTIVATION VERSUS INTRINSIC MOTIVATION

Motivation is found both extrinsically and intrinsically.

Extrinsic motivation exists outside the individual. Usually, it involves the motivation to pursue exterior rewards or trophies—things resulting from successes involving other people. Therefore, extrinsic motivation involves motivation from peers; it involves impressing others via one's success. One's competitive desire can drive this extrinsic motivation completely.

Intrinsic motivation, on the other hand, exists internally. The internal gratification of completing a very personal project, for example, fuels this intrinsic motivation. Perhaps one wants to finish cleaning and decorating one's bedroom simply to feel the fresh, open understanding that one's habitat is for one's self; one's habitat reflects one's life, after all. However, if one simply wants to decorate one's room in order to impress another person, this could deem extrinsic motivation. Essentially, if one is the sole operator of one's motivation without exterior benefit, one is fueled with intrinsic motivation.

A LIFE WITHOUT MOTIVATION: WHAT HAPPENS?

What happens without that pulsing drive of motivation? Where does this lack of motivation lead? Remember that motivation is the building block for all survival, all strength in existence. Furthermore, it is the real push behind desire and interest. It is the very thing that fuels the beautiful paintings in museums, the towering skyscrapers, and the countless football games. It is human's driving force toward the meaning of life.

FEELINGS OF FAILURE AND INADEQUACY

Without motivation, one cannot move forward with one's life. One must remain stagnant. Essentially, one's hometown becomes one's only town. One's first job becomes one's only job. Lack of motivation leads nowhere.

But this lack of push does not lead to a lack of feeling. Emotion is always at play. In fact, emotion is generally the pulse behind lack of motivation. These emotions come in forms like fear of failure, fear of the unknown, incredible stresses, and low self-esteem. If one cannot work through these emotions, one cannot build a solid motivational ground. And without this ground and garnered goals, failure and inadequacy sweep into the emotional mix. One can feel a loss: like the past few years of one's life went toward nothing. One can feel a desire to do it all over again—with that drive of motivation at their backs. Unfortunately, lost years don't come back around. And inadequacy and feelings of failure linger.

Fortunately, these feelings of inadequacy can be the very reason to push toward motivation and reach toward something else. Proper use of feelings is always important. Work toward the promotion you haven't even dreamed about; wonder why you never thought to go to the gym. Understand that there's a whole world out there waiting for you. Claim it.

Chapter 2. Theories of Motivation

Psychologists' motivation analysis involves several theories. They analyze the precise reasons why one is fueled with motivation—and why one may have difficulty jumping on the motivation train.

Drive Theory

Behaviorist Clark Hull created the drive reduction theory of motivation in the 1940s and 1950s. He was one of the first scientists to attempt to understand the broad depth of human motivation.

Homeostasis: Balance and Equilibrium

Hull's theories attend to the facts of homeostasis. Homeostasis is the fact that one's body constantly works to achieve balance, equilibrium. For example, one's body finds a consistent, approximate temperature of 98.6 degrees Fahrenheit. When one dips below or above this number, one's body hustles to achieve balance once more.

Essentially, the "drive" of drive theory refers to the tension aroused by the imbalance or lack of homeostasis in one's body. In the temperature case, therefore, one's interior drive is the fact that one's temperature is out of whack. Further drives are hunger and thirst. These drives, or stimuli, force one's body into action to achieve balance in the form of a meal or a glass of water.

Therefore, Hull's drive theory acts on a sort of stimulus-response mechanism. His theory is rooted in biology and therefore takes no notice of interior, life goals. However, he does provide a decent understanding of the root of motivation.

INSTINCT THEORY

Psychologist William McDougall studied the instinct theory in relation to human motivation. His essential findings rooted the instinct theory as a way through life—a way that assured continuation of life via natural selection. Of course, the behaviors he studied were not limited to biological needs. He studied human instinct; and human instinct garners several shades of gray.

WHAT IS AN INSTINCT?

An instinct involves a tendency to behave in a specific manner without engaging in thought. The acts are spontaneous, occurring in a sort of matter of course after a particular occurrence.

Human instincts cover a broad range of occurrences rooted in both physiological and psychological needs. Physiological motivations, of course, meet hunger, thirst, and habitation needs. Psychological motivations, however, clasp something a bit more human; things like: humor, curiosity, cleanliness, fear, anger, shame, and love.

MASLOW'S HIERARCHY OF NEEDS

Abraham Maslow's humanistic theory of motivation analyzes all the basic human elements—from the simplistic biological needs to the self-actualization needs.

He breaks these needs into five stages with the idea that one's motivations can only escalate when one's needs are met at the immediate stages.

STAGE 1: PHYSIOLOGICAL NEEDS

As aforementioned, physiological needs consist of the basic, survival needs like water, food, and sleep. One must meet these physiological needs prior to building the motivation to move to the next step.

STAGE 2: SAFETY NEEDS

These safety needs involve providing one's self with proper health, income, and an actual "home."

STAGE 3: LOVE/BELONGING NEEDS

After one meets physiological needs and one has a place to live, a place in which to feel whole, one can begin to understand the benefits of social surroundings. These benefits can fall from familial ties, friendship, work groups—anything that forms a sort of relationship in which one can beat back against loneliness and find a place in society.

Stage 4: Self-Esteem Needs

One jumps to the self esteem needs stage in the convenient stage after one feels a sense of belonging. Learning that one "fits" in a society is a great link in the chain. Self-esteem needs allow one the motivation to achieve in one's school or work and to build one's reputation. It allows one to take responsibility of other things or other people. This is essential in the hierarchy of needs: that one does not "need" anything anymore— one is motivated, instead, to help other people meet their needs. One is further motivated to meet one's wants.

Stage 5: Self-Actualization Needs

Self-actualization involves something a bit deeper than the self-esteem stage. The self-esteem stage requires one to achieve in society, to take charge of one's self and one's life. However, the self-actualization stage motivates one to find personal growth, it motivates one to feel fulfilled by one's career, one's relationships. It might not be enough, for example, for one to simply achieve at one's job. This stage might require one to feel as if one's commitment to one's job is also making the world a better place, for example. One might do some soul-searching in this stage to truly understand one's place in the world. One cannot commit to this true soul-searching, of course, without meeting the initial four stages of the hierarchy of needs. However, to truly find one's self and truly meet one's goals, one must exist at this top stage— with all other needs completed.

MOTIVATION:

GETTING MOTIVATED, FEELING MOTIVATED, STAYING MOTIVATED

ONE LAST THING...

If you enjoyed this book or found it useful I'd be very grateful if you'd post a short review on Amazon. Your support really does make a difference and I read all the reviews personally so I can get your feedback and make this book even better.

Thanks again for your support!

10347252R00038

Printed in Great Britain
by Amazon.co.uk, Ltd.,
Marston Gate.